Bar Mitzvah, Bat Mitzvah

Bar Mitzvah, Bat Mitzvah

The Ceremony, the Party, and How the Day Came to Be

by **Bert Metter**

Illustrated by **Joan Reilly**

Clarion Books

New York

Clarion Books
a Houghton Mifflin Company imprint
215 Park Avenue South, New York, NY 10003
Text copyright © 1984, 2007 by Bert Metter
Illustrations copyright © 2007 by Joan Reilly

Portions of this text were originally published
in different form by Clarion Books as
Bar Mitzvah, Bat Mitzvah: How Jewish Boys and Girls Come of Age,
copyright © 1984 by Bert Metter.

The text was set in 13-point Berkeley Book.

www.clarionbooks.com

Printed in the U.S.A.

Library of Congress Cataloging-in-Publication Data

Metter, Bert.
Bar mitzvah, bat mitzvah : the ceremony, the party,
and how the day came to be / by Bert Metter ; illustrated by Joan Reilly.
p. cm.
"Portions of this text were originally published as Bar mitzvah,
bat mitzvah : how Jewish boys and girls come of age,
copyright (c) 1984 by Bert Metter"—T.p. verso.
Includes bibliographical references and index.
ISBN-13: 978-0-618-76772-4
ISBN-10: 0-618-76772-X
1. Bar mitzvah—Juvenile literature. 2. Bat mitzvah—Juvenile literature.
I. Reilly, Joan. II. Title.
BM707.M45 2007
296.4'424—dc22   2006032942

CL ISBN-13: 978-0-618-76772-4   CL ISBN-10: 0-618-76772-X
PA ISBN-13: 978-0-618-76773-1   PA ISBN-10: 0-618-76773-8

WOZ 10 9 8 7 6 5 4 3 2 1

For Alex, Brian, Chase, Jeff, Laura, Lianne, and Riley

—B.M.

For my parents, my husband, and "Uncle Samuel"

—J.R.

The author would like to thank Rabbi Mitchel Hurvitz
of Temple Shalom, Greenwich, Connecticut,
Rabbi Dr. Robert Rothman of Rye Brook, New York,
and Rabbi Daniel Gropper of Community Synagogue
in Rye, New York, for their kind help and suggestions
during the preparation of this book.

Contents

A Note from the Author

This short book has a long history.

I first became curious about bar mitzvahs when my sons had their ceremonies back in the early 1980s. I went to the library searching for a brief, clear, explanatory book. There was none. I was busy writing commercials for Ford, Goodyear, and Kodak at the time, but I did the research, wrote a book, and Clarion Books published it.

Now my sons' children are having ceremonies. The essentials haven't changed, but the world certainly has. Diversity has grown. At a ceremony today, the audience is likely to be filled with many more non-Jewish friends and guests. Hallmark now offers about twenty different greeting cards for bar and bat mitzvahs. There has even been a Hollywood movie, *Keeping Up with the Steins,* centered on bar mitzvah parties. Bat mitzvahs and adult ceremonies have become much more common.

I thought a new explanatory book—written for today's readers and with fresh illustrations—was needed. My publisher, Clarion Books, agreed. I hope you do, too.

CHAPTER ONE

Your Day

YOU GO TO BED EARLY because the next day is a big day, a day when every eye will be on you.

But you don't go to sleep right away because you are thinking about a lot of things.

You lie in bed, and in your mind you go over the prayers that you are to read tomorrow. And you recite lines from the speech you will have to give.

The rabbi said you are going to do just fine. Your parents said you are going to do just fine. Everybody said you are going to do just fine.

But maybe they think you *aren't* going to do just fine. Maybe they only want you to feel good. They probably tell all the kids they're going to do just fine. . . .

You are up early.

And you arrive at the temple early.

The rabbi talks to you for a few minutes—words of encouragement.

Then you go into the sanctuary with your mother and father.

Soon it is crowded.

You see faces you know. Aunts. Uncles. Cousins. Friends. It seems the whole world is there.

You sit quietly and try to relax.

The service begins. The sound of talking changes to the sound of prayers.

The rabbi and the congregation pray. The rabbi reads. The congregation responds. Back and forth. Rabbi. Congregation. Rabbi. Congregation. You can feel the rhythm of the service. The cantor sings. The choir sings. The pages of the prayer book turn, and the service flows.

Now the rabbi walks to the ark, the special cabinet where the Torah scrolls are kept. The curtains are pulled apart, and the rabbi carefully lifts the Torah scrolls out— the scrolls with their words from the Bible. The words have been passed down from more than 5,700 years ago. They are not words printed on paper. The words on the Torah scroll have been carefully hand-lettered on parchment by a scribe using a quill. It took about a year for the scribe to hand-letter that scroll.

Now your relatives are called up—honored—one by one, to recite the Torah blessings.

Then it is your turn.

You walk to the lectern.

The rabbi is no longer leading the congregation in

prayer. Your relatives have finished reciting. The cantor is not singing.

Everyone is looking at you.

You don't concentrate on the faces, but on the prayers.

You recite a blessing. Then you read your passages from the Torah, the Bible passages, the words you have been studying. It is quiet, but you don't notice.

Then that part is over. You have done it. You have stood as an adult and prayed in front of the congregation.

Your parents then say their special prayer. They give thanks for your moral graduation. In a religious sense, you are now responsible for yourself. Your parents will still tell you plenty, as they usually do, about what's right and what's not. But an obligation has passed from them to you.

Then it is time for your speech.

You look at the congregation, at all the people watching you.

And you begin. Once more, you say the words you have worked on. You make comments on your passage from the Torah and express your feelings about what this day means to you.

Then that part is over, too.

You sit off to the side as the service continues.

Finally, the congregation rises, and you walk with the rabbi to the ark to return the Torah scrolls to their place.

The rabbi turns to you and welcomes you now as a *bar mitzvah* or a *bat mitzvah*, a son of the commandment or a daughter of the commandment, a full member of the congregation.

You help the rabbi close the curtains that cover the ark.

The choir sings the closing hymn.

The service is over.

You have done it!

You stand in the receiving line with your parents. There is enough handshaking and hugging and kissing to last you a thousand years.

And then it is time for the celebration. The party. Your friends. Food. Gifts. Music. Fun.

That night, you don't go to bed very early.

But you go to bed very tired.

Images from the day flash through your mind. A lot happened. It has been a special day, a birthday to remember.

And, somehow, you feel more than just a day older.

How the Ceremony Came to Be

BAR MITZVAH. BAT MITZVAH.

How did they begin?

Why are they done the way they are done?

Down through history, many groups of people have had rituals to mark the time when a boy becomes a man and a girl becomes a woman.

Bar mitzvah, which means "son of the commandment," and bat mitzvah, which means "daughter of the commandment," are the ways the Jewish people mark the coming of age of their children.

It is the time when a child becomes responsible for following the rules of Jewish life—the commandments. And it is the time when a child steps up and becomes a full-fledged member of the Jewish community.

But the bar and bat mitzvah ceremonies did not come straight from the Bible. They did not always exist as we know them today. They were created to fill a need—they evolved and grew.

Ancient Ways

Coming-of-age rites go back to a time even before the beginning of the Jewish religion.

Sociologists have recorded the rites of passage of tribes and cultures from all parts of the world. These rites reflected the life and the hopes of the people who practiced them.

Before initiation into a tribe, boys and girls usually had to undergo some sort of test. After they had done this, an elaborate ceremony celebrated their coming of age.

The ceremony of the Karimojong, a Ugandan tribe, involved a child participating in the spearing, cooking, and eating of an ox. This was done in the hope that the child would one day own many cattle and lead a long life.

The rituals of certain ancient tribes of central North America revolved around strength in warfare. For example, boys might have to drag heavy weights attached to their chests or legs.

In the interior of British Columbia, tribal ceremonies were related to future occupations. Boys rolled stones downhill and raced them to the bottom, hoping to grow into fleet-footed warriors. Girls dropped stones inside their dresses so that when they reached childbearing age, their babies would be born as easily as a pebble drops to the ground.

Historians tell us that in ancient times it was most common for boys and girls to be initiated into a tribe between the ages of twelve and fourteen.

This was natural. It is the time when humans usually begin to reach sexual maturity.

Turning Point

When Jewish history began, initiation ceremonies like these were probably common. But the Jewish people changed the emphasis of their coming-of-age rites. The rites became more of a spiritual, and less of a physical, experience.

Ancient Jewish law set twenty as one key age of maturity. That was when a man was expected to pay taxes and go to fight if there was a war.

But for other purposes, the rabbis fixed the age of responsibility at thirteen for boys and twelve for girls (since girls usually mature physically earlier).

Those were the "turning point" ages.

Girls were treated differently in the synagogue, too. Women did not take part in prayer services, as men did. There were separate sections in synagogues for women. They sat apart, sometimes in balconies. At a bar mitzvah

ceremony, women might throw candy down as part of the celebration when a boy finished his Torah reading.

Young men and women moved through childhood and youth at a much faster pace back then. The custom was for children to begin studying the Bible when they first learned to read. They began work earlier. They were often married by the time they were fifteen. Many were advanced enough in religious studies to take part in services—to come of age—before they were thirteen. And that was fine. There was no rule or custom to hold them back.

They were expected to live up to the commandments as soon as they could understand them.

But thirteen was the official age. At that age, it was your duty to follow the commandments.

By thirteen, your vow was considered a valid vow—and you were held to it.

By thirteen, your word became acceptable in a court of law.

By thirteen, you were expected to fast on the Jewish Day of Atonement, Yom Kippur, just as an adult was expected to do.

When you were thirteen, you were taken to an elder rabbi of the community. The rabbi blessed you and prayed you would follow the commandments. There were no bar mitzvahs or bat mitzvahs as we know them today. Since many children younger than thirteen had

already been taking part in services, there was no need for a special ceremony.

Beginning of the Tradition

About seven hundred years ago, during the Middle Ages, some Jewish communities in Northern Europe changed their attitudes about children taking part in services. It was felt that before thirteen you were too young to really understand the meaning of what was happening. The practice of the very young participating in services was discouraged.

Gradually, the custom of waiting until your thirteenth birthday became accepted. This made your thirteenth birthday an important occasion, not just another birthday.

And so a thirteenth-birthday ceremony evolved. Over the years, it grew into the kind of bar mitzvah ceremony we have today.

The ceremony was for boys only, not for girls.

But then, on the afternoon of March 18, 1922, that changed.

CHAPTER THREE

Judith Steps Up

JUDITH KAPLAN FELT NERVOUS but also determined. She had left her mother, her grandmothers, and her sisters in the narrow rear room with the other women. She walked into the wider front room, where only the men sat. Many eyes followed her.

She took her place: one small twelve-year-old girl, sitting among many men.

She knew she should concentrate on the prayers and Torah reading she would have to recite. But she could not help thinking about the stir she was creating. She knew that many of the people in the congregation felt she should not be sitting there. Both her grandmothers were against her breaking the tradition they had known for their entire lives.

She was at the center of a sharp controversy.

But there was no use worrying about that now.

Women's Rites

The year was 1922, and there had never been a bat mitzvah in the United States.

There had also never been a woman senator or governor or Supreme Court justice. Harvard, Yale, and Princeton did not accept female students.

But things were changing. Nineteen months earlier, the U.S. Constitution had been amended to give women the right to vote.

Judith's father, Rabbi Mordecai Kaplan, who would start the Jewish Reconstructionist Movement, believed women should be more involved in the rites of their religion. He believed girls should have a coming-of-age ceremony, just as boys did. He felt it was the right thing, that this was the right time, and that Judith was the right girl.

He nodded to his daughter. She stood up but did not go to the platform. Women did not do that then.

Judith read her prayers and her selection from the Torah, first in Hebrew, then in English. And then she sat down. The Torah scroll was put back in the ark, and the service ended.

Judith sighed in relief. No thunder had sounded; no lightning had struck. Everything seemed normal.

But much had changed. The first bat mitzvah in the United States had taken place, and a new tradition had begun.

And it grew. Over the years, a bat mitzvah became essentially the same as a bar mitzvah. Today, bat mitzvah ceremonies are common in Reform, Conservative, and Reconstructionist congregations throughout the world. And there are parallel celebrations in many modern Orthodox congregations.

Rabbi Sally

Another young girl also helped change Jewish religious traditions. In 1961, when she was sixteen, Sally Priesand began to have strong feelings about her goal in life. Sally decided she wanted to become a rabbi.

After many years of study, work, and controversy,

Sally became the first woman in America to be ordained as a rabbi by a major Jewish denomination.

Today, there are hundreds of women rabbis—Reform, Conservative, and Reconstructionist—across the country.

Reliving History

Despite her controversial bat mitzvah, Judith Kaplan aspired to make music, not news. She studied at what is now the Juilliard School, took graduate studies, and earned a PhD; was married and had two daughters; taught, composed, and published Jewish music.

When she turned eighty-two, Judith Kaplan Eisenstein celebrated with a second bat mitzvah.

This time, when she read her Torah section, she stood up on the platform next to the Torah scroll. She was surrounded by other women on the platform, many of them well known, who had gathered from around the country to honor her.

And, unlike that anxious day in 1922, this time Judith was smiling.

CHAPTER FOUR

The Ceremony

AT THE CENTER OF THE JEWISH RELIGION are the first five books of the Bible. These five books make up the Law of Moses, the Teaching, or, in Hebrew, the Torah. The Torah, inscribed on a scroll, is at the focal point of every synagogue. And it is at the heart of the bar and bat mitzvah ceremonies.

In the ceremony, the young man or woman is called up to the Torah to read from it and from other parts of the Bible relating to it. Then the parents offer a prayer of thanks that this day has come to be. Finally, the young man or woman gives a speech about the meaning of the Torah and this day. It all begins with the Teaching.

The Teaching

The Torah has influenced a great part of the human race. In Christianity, the five books are considered holy and are part of the Old Testament. In Islam, these books are considered divinely inspired. But the relationship of the Jewish people to the Torah is special and different.

These books begin with the story of creation: "In the beginning God created the heaven and the earth. . . ." They tell of the birth of the Jewish people—the agreement, called the covenant, between God and Abraham: "I will establish my covenant between me and you, and your offspring after you. . . ." They include the laying down of the Ten Commandments, the essence of Jewish morality, the written law. The five books conclude with the death of Moses.

The bar and bat mitzvah ceremonies mark a new relationship between young men and women and these sacred Jewish books. From the time they are called up, they are personally responsible for living up to the Teaching.

The Scrolls and the Ark

In every synagogue, in front of the congregation, are the Torah scrolls. They are kept in an enclosure, or a cabinet, called the ark. There are usually ceremonial curtains draped around the ark, and a light that is never turned off hangs above it.

The scrolls are considered sacred. They are made the same way they were thousands of years ago: a trained scribe writes them in Hebrew on parchment (animal skin, usually that of a calf or a cow). The scribe uses a quill (a bird feather, usually from a turkey) and can hand-letter a little more than a page a day. It takes about a year to create a Torah.

The scrolls are treated with the greatest respect. When they are removed from the ark or returned to it, the congregation stands. The scroll is not to be touched directly by anyone's hands. A pointer is used to follow the words. When the ark is opened or closed, prayers are chanted.

The scrolls and the ark go back to the beginning of Jewish history. In biblical times, the ark was a portable chest. The Bible tells how the commandments received by Moses from God were inscribed on tablets of stone. The tablets were carried in the ark by the Jews as they marched from Egypt, searching for a homeland.

The ark with the commandments led the procession.

It proclaimed who the Jews were: they were the people who carried God's word. This made them feel strong and protected by God.

Whenever they lifted the ark to start their journey or put it down when they came to rest, Moses said a special prayer.

When the Jews settled in Jerusalem and the First Temple was built, the ark containing the commandments was kept in the Temple.

Eventually, it became the custom to build an ark for the Torah permanently into the wall of every synagogue.

And that's where we see the ark today.

It is built so that when we face it, we look toward Jerusalem, the site of the first Jewish temple.

When the scrolls are removed from the ark, or returned to it, the congregation rises. When the ark is opened or closed, prayers are chanted, just as Moses said prayers when the ark was carried forward or put down at rest on the march from Egypt.

The bar and bat mitzvah ceremonies call a young man or woman up to the ark and the scrolls—the Teaching—and to new responsibility.

Going Up

Every service is built around the reading of a particular part of the Torah.

The Torah is hundreds of pages long. It is divided up

Simchat Torah

so that during a year of services the entire Torah is read through once.

The readings proceed like the seasons of the year. Special Torah readings mark off the Jewish holidays.

Each year at the end of the cycle there is a joyous celebration, *Simchat Torah* (Rejoicing in the Law), and the scrolls are paraded through the synagogue.

At a bar or bat mitzvah ceremony service, as at every service, the scrolls are removed from the ark and placed on a stand for reading. There are prayers and blessings before and after the Torah is removed from the ark:

"We praise you, Eternal God. Sovereign of the Universe:
You have called us to Your service by giving us the Torah.
We praise you, O God, Giver of the Torah. . . ."

There is the reading from that week's portion of the Torah. And there are readings from other parts of the Bible related to that week's Torah portion.

Various members of the congregation are honored by being called up to take part in these readings. This honor is called an *aliyah* in Hebrew—a "going up."

An *aliyah* can be used to mark many special occasions. You may be called up before or after your marriage. You may be called up after the birth of a child. And you are called up to mark your coming of age.

When you are called up to the Torah for the first time, you are making a spiritual ascent. You are being called up to begin a new relationship with God's Teaching.

From this time forward, you are a participant. Responsible. Accountable.

On the day of your bar or bat mitzvah ceremony, you take part in the service in an active way. Your part may be large or small. You may read blessings before or after the Torah readings. You may read part, or all, of that day's portion of the Teaching. You may chant other parts of the Bible related to that day's Torah portion or read other portions of the worship service. Your role depends on your ambition, your ability, and on the custom of your congregation.

The chanting heard during a service follows ancient melodies. Words in the Hebrew Bible have markings that guide the way they are chanted.

And so the ceremony brings you into the service, into the congregation, and into the Jewish religion in your new role.

On Your Shoulders

When adult Jews pray formally, they drape a prayer shawl, called a *tallit* in Hebrew, over their shoulders. The shawl has specially knotted fringes as reminders of the many commandments to be followed. You are given a prayer shawl either shortly before your coming-of-age ceremony or at the ceremony, according to the custom of your congregation.

In ancient days, a sick child might have been wrapped

Tallit

in a *tallit* while a parent prayed for speedy recovery. At Jewish wedding ceremonies today, the bride and groom often stand under a canopy, which may be a large *tallit*.

Another practice of personal prayer is the wearing of *tefillin*. These are small leather cases containing Torah passages written on tiny pieces of parchment. One is wrapped around your arm, another on your forehead. This follows passages in the Bible:

> *"You shall put these, my words,*
> *on your heart and on your soul,*
> *and you shall bind them for signs on your hands*
> *and they shall be as frontlets between your eyes."*

Tefillin are worn during the morning prayer service, except on the Sabbath and most Jewish holidays.

When community prayer services are held, there is a requirement that at least ten worshipers be present. Ten is a quorum, or a *minyan* in Hebrew. In most non-Orthodox synagogues today, women may be counted as part of a *minyan*.

From the day of your bar or bat mitzvah on, you count as part of a *minyan*, too.

The Parents' Prayer

Traditionally, there is a prayer said at the ceremony by one or both of your parents. Up until your thirteenth (or twelfth) year, they have been responsible for your moral behavior.

Until now, you may not have truly understood the difference between right and wrong. You were too young to absorb the meaning of the Teaching.

Your moral slate is, theoretically, still clean. But that time is ending.

Now you are becoming a son or daughter of the Torah. And for this, your parents give thanks:

"Blessed be thou, O Lord, our God,
King of the Universe, who has kept us in life,
Sustained us, and enabled us to reach
this joyous occassion . . ."

In orthodox congregations, the parents' prayer gives thanks for being freed from moral responsibility for their child.

Tefillin

Parents' prayers express happiness that a son or daughter is ready to enter the religious community. Now, at last, the child is ready to accept responsibility for following the commandments.

But the Jewish religion is family-minded. The obligation of your parents to guide you continues.

And your obligation to your parents never ends, as the commandments make clear: *"Honor your father and mother. . . ."*

The Jewish religion is also practical. It teaches that parents prepare their children for accepting new responsibilities. You should be ready to step up.

The Stage Is Yours

Most of a bar or bat mitzvah ceremony is designed to bring you into the flow of the service. You blend in. You are being absorbed by the congregation.

But there is also a part in which you can express yourself as an individual: your speech. Traditionally, there is a short discourse—the Hebrew word is *dereshah*—in which you comment on the portion of the Teaching read at the service.

Your speech can be prepared with guidance from a rabbi, religious teacher, or parent. It gives you a chance to describe your feelings as you step over the threshold to religious maturity.

The practice of commenting on Jewish holy writing

goes back to the early days of the religion. From ancient times, rabbis and scholars would take biblical verses and analyze them. The tradition of interpreting the Scriptures guided the growth of Jewish sacred writings.

But where do thirteen-year-olds come in?

Jewish children of the past lived in a far different world than we do. About five hundred years ago, European Jews were forced into ghettos. They could not travel freely, and they were limited in the work they could do.

Religion helped sustain them; it played a central role in their lives.

There were few diversions for children: no TV, no video games, no computers or Internet. And no public schools. But there were religious schools—and plenty of religious study.

By the time children reached thirteen, they could be skilled in commenting on portions of the Bible. The brightest could discuss and analyze the meaning of a biblical passage.

And so the custom grew for children to give a speech on the portion of the Teaching read at the service when they turned thirteen.

This was often done in their home at a reception after the service. Relatives and friends would be invited to see the new son of the commandment display his knowledge.

Then, many years later, ghetto walls started coming

down. Life became more open for Jews, and religious study became less all-consuming. Yet the tradition of giving a speech at the time of your coming-of-age continued—and does to this day.

Usually, the young man or woman thanks his or her parents and teachers. And they express the hope that the lessons of the Torah will be applied wisely in the years ahead.

After your speech, the rabbi will usually say a few words to you. The rabbi will bless you and pray that you will follow the commandments and serve God.

Finally, the scrolls have been returned, the ark has been closed, the prayers have all been said. The service ends, having gone like most other services through the years.

Except that at this one, you passed a milestone.

And now it's time to celebrate.

CHAPTER FIVE

Party Time

THE TRADITION OF A BAR OR BAT MITZVAH PARTY had a simple, practical beginning. It originated in the days when the ceremony was first starting to take shape. After the service, relatives and neighbors wanted to gather and discuss the big day. And so parents would host a dinner at their home.

This gave their son an audience so he could display his religious knowledge with a speech. Eventually, the speech became part of the ceremony at the synagogue.

Bash vs. Basic

Today, there are widely different ways to celebrate the joy of the event. And that's natural. Jewish parents and their sons or daughters have widely different personalities, and means.

Not long ago, a famous rapper and an award-winning R&B singer, Ja Rule and Ashanti, both performed at a glittering bat mitzvah with hundreds of guests. The party made news.

Meanwhile, in a small-town ceremony in Alabama, a young man had his bar mitzvah with a traveling rabbi who serves twenty-eight temples with small congregations. The party was what the young man wanted: refreshments at the synagogue.

People at both events enjoyed themselves.

The Right Balance

Ever since biblical days, rabbis and families have struggled for a balance between the urge to celebrate and the need for restraint.

Religious laws, called sumptuary regulations, were created to keep the lid on.

Rabbis pointed out that excesses were not right spiritually. Besides, Jews were a minority in most communities. They did not want to stir up envy or anger among their non-Jewish neighbors.

In Italy, about five hundred years ago, rabbis ruled that there would be a tax on every guest over a fixed limit. To keep taxes down, your guest list had to be kept in check.

In Poland, there was a decree that limited the jewelry that could be worn: two rings on weekdays, four on weekends, six on holidays.

At one time or another, there were restrictions on what kind of clothing could be worn, how many courses could be served at the meal, and what kind of gifts could be given.

All these rules were designed to keep celebrations within bounds. The rabbis felt a party marking a religious event should not wander too far from a religious spirit. And that's still the feeling today.

Of course, after much study and preparation, it's natural to want to have a little fun. Besides, there's a lot of emotion wrapped up in the occasion.

It celebrates your religious coming-of-age.

It celebrates your becoming a teenager (or, for girls of twelve, close to it).

It affirms a commitment to Judaism.

And it happens once in a lifetime.

Mazel tov! Enjoy.

CHAPTER SIX

Late to the Party

THROUGH THE YEARS, the traditional age of passage has always been thirteen (actually, thirteen and a day) for boys and twelve for girls. But recently a new tradition has taken hold: the adult bar and bat mitzvah.

This practice began to become popular after Judith Kaplan stood up at the first bat mitzvah ceremony in America in 1922. Women who hadn't had the opportunity when they were young wanted to go up, read from the Torah, and affirm their faith. And so many had adult bat mitzvahs.

Catching Up

Over time, others—men and women who had not been ready or willing when they were young—also began having adult ceremonies.

A West Point cadet who had missed his bar mitzvah when he was thirteen had it at the age of twenty-one at Eisenhower Hall at the Military Academy.

A Long Island businessman, whose parents tried to flee the Nazis but died in a concentration camp, had a ceremony at the age of fifty-six to help rekindle his Jewish identity.

A medical writer in Manhattan had a ceremony twenty-four years after her son's bar mitzvah. She had skipped her ceremony as a girl and felt a spiritual void.

Of course, just wanting the ceremony is one thing. Undertaking the study and Hebrew lessons is something else: a serious commitment. Yet today, adult bar and bat mitzvahs are common in many congregations.

Twice Blessed

There are also people who decide to restate their faith with a second ceremony. The actor Kirk Douglas, father of actor Michael Douglas, had been in a helicopter crash that almost killed him. A few years later, he had a stroke, but again survived. He was grateful for being alive. *Thank God,* he thought. Yes, thank God. . . . But how?

Douglas said, "In the Torah, it is written that a man's life span is seventy years. After that, he begins all over again. I am eighty-three years old—thirteen years after seventy. So I am thirteen again. I will thank God by having my second bar mitzvah."

His friends thought he was joking. But he studied his Hebrew prayers and did it.

In his speech, he said, "You know, this old *tallis*—the

prayer shawl I'm wearing—I wore on my first bar mitzvah seventy years ago. And if my mother is looking down and watching us, she will recognize it."

Like a traditional bar and bat mitzvah, adult ceremonies usually have a celebration afterward. These may not be as lively as a twelve- or thirteen-year-old's, but they are always heartfelt.

Evan and Daryl Sabara

From Star Trek to Spy Kids

NOTHING IS MORE PERSONAL than your ceremony. It reflects your unique character and style as well as the beliefs of your parents and your congregation.

But it is also a rite of passage you share with many others.

Some of the movie and TV stars and athletes that you watch and admire (or don't admire) have gone through the same challenges and pleasures you will face.

Star Trek's Captain Kirk (William Shatner), commander of the starship *Enterprise*, is Jewish. So is his co-star, Mr. Spock (Leonard Nimoy). Shatner had a traditional bar mitzvah ceremony in Montreal, Canada, where he was brought up.

The "Spy Kids," twin brothers Evan and Daryl Sabara, had a double ceremony. The Sabara brothers have been in three *Spy Kids* movies, the film *Her Best Move,* the television show *Malcolm in the Middle,* and more. Evan says, "I didn't want a big party or anything. We just wanted it to be meaningful. Our Torah portion was about someone who is fortunate and tries to give a helping hand to others. That's the way I try to live my life." The table centerpieces at their party were bundles of books, from *Tom Sawyer* to *Fahrenheit 451,* which were donated to their school for reading courses.

Academy Award–winning director Steven Spielberg felt a little let down the day after his bar mitzvah ceremony. He still had to go to bed at nine o'clock. That didn't quite seem to go with the previous day's proclamation: "Today you are a man and forever you shall be."

The Unexpected

Of course, sometimes a ceremony doesn't go quite as planned. Zoe Weizenbaum is a young actress balancing high school and a movie career (she has appeared in *Twelve and Holding* and *Memoirs of a Geisha*). Her bat mitzvah date had to be shifted because of filming work. Since your Torah reading depends on the day your service takes place, she had to learn two different Torah readings, not just one.

This was no problem for Zoe, though. Her rabbi said she chanted beautifully. And her speech, which was on what being Jewish means to her, was one of the best he ever heard.

Richard Lewis, a comedian who has appeared on

Zoe Weizenbaum

Comedy Central as well as in movies and on TV shows such as *Curb Your Enthusiasm,* also had his bar mitzvah date moved. Richard's father was a prominent kosher caterer. "My father basically did everyone's bar mitzvah who I knew, and the stars' sons' bar mitzvahs," Richard said. Since his father was booked on the week of his bar mitzvah party, Richard celebrated on a Tuesday night instead of on Saturday. But to compensate, the food was unbeatable, he says, and so was the party.

Surprises

Sarah Hughes, who won an Olympic gold medal in figure skating, remembers the bar mitzvah of her brother David. Displayed at the party was a special surprise—the Stanley

Cup, professional hockey's top award. Sarah's dad, a former hockey player, arranged for it to be there.

The actor and comedian Ben Stiller also had something surprising happen at his bar mitzvah celebration. Ben played the drums in his own band at his party. After one number, his father ran up to him, very upset. The song the singer had just belted out was "Hey, Jude" by the Beatles. His father had mistaken it as "Hey, Jew." All was quickly straightened out.

Ben Stiller

Unusual Settings

Ben Foster, who appeared in *X-Men: The Last Stand* with Halle Berry and *Alpha Dog* with Bruce Willis, had his ceremony in a former Catholic church. In Ben's hometown in Iowa, the congregation was small. They put a Jewish star on a renovated church, and that was their temple.

"The ceremony had a profound effect on me," Ben says. "It's a milestone in a man's life, beyond words. Being able to stand up and respect my roots and being able to have my nana and poppa [grandparents] there was a wonderful thing."

The TV and movie actor Jeremy Piven (*Entourage, Black Hawk Down, Scary Movie 3*) had his celebration in nontraditional quarters—his basement. "I was probably the worst Hebrew student of the bunch," Jeremy says, "mostly because at the time I was playing football. . . . I can't believe I even did it and made it."

Even though his ceremony and party were simple, Jeremy looks back on them as perfect.

The Academy Award–nominated actor Jake Gyllenhaal had an even more unusual location for his bar mitzvah party: a homeless shelter. His parents wanted him to be grateful for his privileged lifestyle. And so Jake and his friends spent the day with the kids in the shelter.

Jitters

David Copperfield, one of the world's best-known magicians, is famous for his skill and smooth performances. Yet David was far from confident at his bar mitzvah. "I was sweating with a 102-degree temperature," he recalls. "I had ice cubes on my head because I was so nervous about remembering my *haftarah* [the Torah reading from the books of the Prophets]."

But he got through it. "I'm happy for the experience," he says, "and if I'm lucky enough to have children someday, I'll do the same for them."

Actress Jami Gertz (*Keeping Up with the Steins, Twister, Ally McBeal*) also ran into unexpected problems at her bat mitzvah. She had a 103-degree fever, and there was a snowstorm that prevented half of her relatives from getting to her synagogue in Chicago. "There are pictures of me on three chairs, lying down," she says. "I enjoyed my son's bar mitzvah much more." In a reverse of the usual order, Jami's mother studied and became a bat mitzvah after Jami did.

Mark Spitz is no stranger to performing under pressure. As a competitive swimmer, he climbed the winner's stand seven times at one Olympics to receive a gold medal. Each medal involved setting a new world record. No one had ever done that before.

But Mark was nervous about getting through his bar mitzvah.

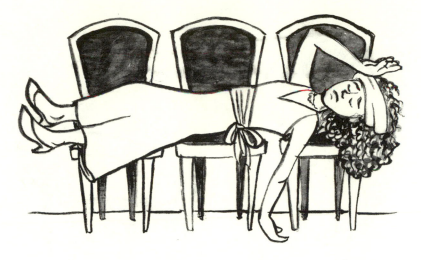

Jami Gertz

He needn't have worried. "There were only two people who knew I made a mistake," he says. "In my *haftarah* portion, I chanted one line twice. Only my grandfather and the rabbi knew that." And they weren't telling.

Modest Beginnings

Larry King's TV interview show, one of the highest rated programs on CNN, has millions of viewers each week. But his Brooklyn bar mitzvah was decidedly low-key.

"The ceremony was bare-bones," he explains. "We were just getting off being on welfare. We didn't have a party. I had the ceremony, and then we served snacks in the anteroom at the synagogue."

Larry King

Norman Lear

David Krumholz

Greg Grunberg

A modest Brooklyn bar mitzvah seems to be a common theme in the lives of young Jewish boys who went on to great success. Norman Lear has produced a long string of TV and movie hits, including *All in the Family* and *The Princess Bride*.

"I remember a bathtub filled with soft drinks and beer and ice," he says. The gifts he recalls were two-dollar bills and a fountain pen.

The actor David Krumholtz (*Numb3rs, ER, The Santa Clause*) also had a modest setting for his bar mitzvah party. "We couldn't afford to rent a hall," he says, "so we had the reception in the synagogue's basement—lox and bagels only." But David rates his prayer readings and speech as a clear success.

Hints of Things to Come

Greg Grunberg, of the TV shows *Alias, Heroes,* and *Felicity,* is an actor who had no qualms about getting up before an audience. "My bar mitzvah was a huge memory for me," he says. "It was exciting, a big challenge. Back then I didn't know I was going to act, but it was a lot of fun. I loved the theatrics of it."

Gene Wilder (*Willy Wonka and the Chocolate Factory, Young Frankenstein*) remembers practicing the chanting of his Torah portion a year before his bar mitzvah. "I was distraught," Gene says, "because I had a high soprano voice and no one could hear me in the temple. I said, 'I'm

Marlee Matlin

not going to be bar mitzvah if you don't have microphones next year.' And they put the microphones in. And then, of course, my voice changed."

Inner Voice

The actress Marlee Matlin, who has starred in *Law & Order, West Wing,* and *Desperate Housewives,* can't hear her own voice; she became deaf before she was two years old. Marlee had to work especially hard preparing for her bat mitzvah.

She remembers: "Every day I worked to phonetically pronounce the Hebrew that would eventually be part of my *haftarah*. By the time my bat mitzvah day had arrived, I was ready. As I read my portion, I looked out at the audience for inspiration. But instead of smiling faces, I saw my mother and father crying. I found out later they couldn't restrain their tears of joy. . . . I started crying, too. . . . Soon everyone was crying. I noticed I had cried on the Torah. I was mortified. The rabbi wiped away my tears and said, 'Your tears are tears of joy and will remind us of your accomplishments.'"

Eight years later, Marlee stood up to speak before another audience. This time it was at the Academy Awards ceremony for winning the Best Actress award for her performance in the movie *Children of a Lesser God*.

Whether or not you ever win an Academy Award, an Olympic gold medal, or some other shining prize, the memory of your bar or bat mitzvah will stay with you for many years.

Top Hats and Candy

JEWS ARE A FAR-FLUNG PEOPLE.

History has dispersed them to all corners of the world.

And so, as the bar and bat mitzvah ceremony spread from country to country, it took on many flavors.

Even within the United States, traditions vary among denominations and congregations.

In some Hasidic communities, it is customary for the audience to interrupt the bar mitzvah speech with comments or questions. This is to set a relaxed mood so the speech goes more easily.

At some temples, the tradition of throwing candy at the boy or girl is followed. This is linked to the ancient practice of throwing grain at a wedding couple (today, rice or birdseed) to wish for fertility and happiness.

William Kristol, editor of the *Weekly Standard,* says, "As a thirteen-year-old, I wore a top hat for my bar mitzvah." His Manhattan synagogue, Shearith Israel, is formal and ornate. Men wore top hats to come to the Torah, as they may still do on special occasions in a few temples in England.

In Other Lands

In Morocco, in northern Africa, there is a tradition of a boy and his father having their hair cut the evening before the bar mitzvah ceremony. Symbolic hair cutting was originally done to children on the day they first entered school.

In traditional bar mitzvah ceremonies in Morocco, you arrive at the synagogue and leave in a procession of family and friends, who often sing and carry candles.

There is an Algerian tradition that involves your two best friends. You choose them as companions, or side-kicks, somewhat like the groomsmen or bridesmaids at a wedding. They sleep over at your house the night before the ceremony and help you get through the day.

In Libya, you go to your mother before leaving for the synagogue to ask forgiveness for any trouble you have caused her during your childhood. She washes your hands to show, symbolically, that she forgives you.

Another Libyan tradition involves inviting any poor or orphaned thirteen-year-old who is ready for his rite of passage the same day as you to join you in the ceremony.

If you live in Tunisia, the evening before the ceremony, your friends gather at your home for a festive meal.

They may also join you in a hair-cutting session. The next day, you are accompanied to the synagogue by family, relatives, friends, and singers.

Traveling to Celebrate

Trips to historic sites are sometimes part of a coming-of-age experience.

Some bar and bat mitzvah celebrants journey to pray at the Western Wall in Jerusalem, which is 2,000 years old and part of the original Second Temple.

Others travel to Masada, a fortress on a high plateau near the Dead Sea, where Jews fought the Romans in ancient times.

Some go to the oldest continually operating synagogue in the Western Hemisphere, Mikve Israel-Emanuel, on Curaçao, a small Dutch island in the Caribbean. The congregation there was established more than one hundred years before the American Revolution.

But no matter where in the world you are, the essential rites remain the same: you step up to the Torah, you accept moral responsibility, and you celebrate.

CHAPTER NINE

Up, Up, and Away

OF ALL JEWISH RITUALS, THE BAR MITZVAH and bat mitzvah ceremonies have grown especially popular and more elaborate over the years.

Why?

Taking part in the ceremony doesn't make you Jewish.

Children born of a Jewish mother are considered Jewish.

Males enter the Jewish covenant with God by being circumcised when they are eight days old.

And you automatically become responsible for obeying the commandments when you are a boy of thirteen or a girl of twelve. This is so whether or not you have a bar or bat mitzvah ceremony.

Yet the ceremony has filled a need. It has evolved, spread throughout the world, grown stronger.

It's a time when you stand up on your own in front of your family, your friends, and your congregation and accept the Jewish teaching.

For many people, traditional religion is not woven into daily life as much as it was in the past. And that may be why standing up and affirming your faith seems so important and has increased in popularity.

The ceremony is valuable for other reasons, too.

As boys and girls grow, they begin to face moral questions. The religious study encouraged by and required for the ceremony helps prepare them for facing these questions.

And, in a way, a bar or bat mitzvah ceremony sets a pattern for meeting many of life's challenges.

You prepare yourself—as you do when studying for the ceremony.

You take a deep breath, stand up, and do the job—as you do at the service.

And, when you're lucky, you enjoy your accomplishment—as you do at your party.

That's when you can say, "I did it."

Congratulations.

You're on your way.

Selected Bibliography

Books and Periodicals

Douglas, Kirk. *My Stroke of Luck.* New York: HarperCollins, 2002.

Eisenberg, Azriel, ed. *Eyewitness to American Jewish History. Part 4: The American Jew, 1915–1969.* New York: URJ Press, 1981.

Elfman, Lois. "Sarah Hughes—Golden Opportunities." *Lifestyles Magazine,* February 2005.

Goldberg, Jennifer. "Comedian Richard Lewis Speaks His Mind." *Jewish News of Greater Phoenix,* vol. 56, no. 38, June 11, 2004.

Marcus, Ivan G. *The Jewish Life Cycle: Rites of Passage from Biblical to Modern Times.* Seattle: University of Washington Press, 2004.

Miller, Gerri. "Foster Reaches for the 'Heights.'" *JVibe Magazine,* online edition.

————. "My Big Fat Jewish Bar Mitzvah." *American Jewish Life Magazine,* May/June 2006.

Oppenheimer, Mark. *Thirteen and a Day: The Bar and Bat Mitzvah Across America.* New York: Farrar, Strauss, and Giroux, 2005.

Oseary, Guy. *Jews Who Rock*. New York: St. Martin's, 2001.

Ouaknin, Marc-Alain, and Françoise-Anne Menager. *Bar Mitzvah: A Guide to Spiritual Growth*. New York: Assouline, 2006.

Pfefferman, Naomi. "The Right Type." *The Jewish Journal of Greater Los Angeles*, November 23, 2001.

Pogrebin, Abigail. *Stars of David: Prominent Jews Talk About Being Jewish*. New York: Broadway Books, 2005.

Schauss, Hayyim. *The Lifetime of a Jew: Throughout the Ages of History*. New York: URJ Press, 1950.

Websites

movies.about.com. About.com is an online source of information on practically any topic, with a library of over 1.2 million pieces of original content. The Hollywood Movies section of the site contains articles on many Jewish celebrities.

chabad.com. The website for West Coast Chabad Lubavitch, a community-based nonprofit organization whose efforts are rooted in traditional Jewish values.

juf.org/tweens. This section of the Jewish United Fund/Jewish Federation of Metropolitan Chicago's website was created specifically for kids aged 10–13. It's filled with games, recipes, Jewish celebrities, and tons of good ideas.

jvibe.com. JVibe is a hip, Jewish webzine for teens and by teens. JVibe's content focuses on music, book, and film reviews; Israel trips and other worldly adventures; celebrity profiles; features on teens committed to social action; contests; sports; sexuality; holidays; advice; and making connections with other teens.

keshet.org. Founded in 1982, Keshet provides educational, recreational, and vocational programs for children and young adults with special needs.

netribution.co.uk. Netribution is a British website that features film industry news, resources, interviews, information, and humor.

Source Notes

Chapter 6
Late to the Party

pp. 40–41   "In the Torah . . . second bar mitzvah" and "You know, this . . . she will recognize it" is from *My Stroke of Luck* by Kirk Douglas, pp. 134–35.

Chapter 7
From *Star Trek* to *Spy Kids*

p. 43   The information about William Shatner's bar mitzvah is from *Stars of David: Prominent Jews Talk About Being Jewish* by Abigail Pogrebin, p. 353.

pp. 43–44   "I didn't want . . . try to live my life" is from Bradford Wiss's article "Lights, Action, Bar Mitzvah: The Spy Kids Turn 13," which can be found on the West Coast Chabad Lubavitch website at www.chabad.com/site/c.eeJNIWOzErH/b.1986853/apps/s/content.asp?ct=2846729 (or, just go to www.chabad.com and search for "spy kids").

p. 44   Steven Spielberg's post–bar mitzvah reaction is from *Stars of David: Prominent Jews Talk About Being Jewish* by Abigail Pogrebin, p. 29.

p. 44   The information about Zoe Weizenbaum's bat mitzvah can be found on the Jewish United Fund/Jewish Federation of Metropolitan Chicago's website at www.juf.org/tweens/new_cel.asp?id=105 (or, just go to www.juf.org/tweens/celebrity.asp and scroll down to find Zoe's name).

p. 45 "My father . . . sons' bar mitzvahs" is from Jennifer Goldberg's article "Comedian Richard Lewis Speaks His Mind," which appeared in the *Jewish News of Greater Phoenix* and can be found online at www.jewishaz.com/jewish news/040611/lewis.shtml.

pp. 45–46 Sarah Hughes's memories of her brother's bar mitzvah are recounted in Lois Elfman's article "Sarah Hughes—Golden Opportunities," which appeared in *Lifestyles Magazine* and can be found online at www.lifestylesmagazine.com/Lifestyle_02-2005_004.html.

p. 46 The story of Ben Stiller's bar mitzvah party is from the introduction of *Jews Who Rock* by Guy Oseary.

p. 47 "The ceremony had . . . a wonderful thing" is from Gerri Miller's article about Ben Foster for *JVibe Magazine*, "Foster Reaches for the 'Heights,'" which can be found online at www.jvibe.com/popculture/heights.shtml.

p. 47 "I was probably . . . and made it" is from "Jeremy Piven Talks About *Keeping Up with the Steins*" by Fred Topel, which can be found online at http://movies.about.com/od/keepingupwiththesteins/a/jpi ven051006.htm or by going to http://about.com and searching for "Jeremy Piven interview."

p. 47   The story of Jake Gyllenhaal's bar mitzvah appears in many online sources, including an interview with the actor dated January 27, 2006, "BAFTA Winner Jake Gyllenhaal— Love and War" by Stephen Applebaum, which can be found online at www.netribution.co.uk/2/content/view/86/35.

p. 48   "I was sweating . . . remembering my *haftarah*" and "I'm happy for . . . the same for them" are from *Stars of David: Prominent Jews Talk About Being Jewish* by Abigail Pogrebin, p. 345.

p. 48   "There are pictures . . . mitzvah much more" is from Gerri Miller's article about Jami Gertz for the May/June 2006 issue of *American Jewish Life Magazine*, "My Big Fat Jewish Bar Mitzvah," which can be found online at www.ajlmagazine.com/content/052006/coverstory.html.

p. 49   "There were only . . . rabbi knew that" is from *Stars of David: Prominent Jews Talk About Being Jewish* by Abigail Pogrebin, p. 324.

p. 49   "The ceremony was . . . at the synagogue" is from *Stars of David: Prominent Jews Talk About Being Jewish* by Abigail Pogrebin, p. 321.

p. 51   "I remember a bathtub . . . beer and ice" is from *Stars of David: Prominent Jews Talk About Being Jewish* by Abigail Pogrebin, p. 341.

p. 51   "We couldn't afford . . . and bagels only" is from "The Right Type," an article by Naomi Pfefferman that appeared in the November 23, 2001, issue of *The Jewish Journal of Greater Los Angeles* and can be found online at www.jewishjournal.com/home/preview.php?id=7745.

p. 51 "My bar mitzvah . . . theatrics of it" is from "Haftorah Memories," an article in the May/June 2006 issue of *American Jewish Life Magazine* that can be found online at www.ajlmagazine.com/content/052006/haftorah.

pp. 51–52 "I was distraught . . . my voice changed" is from *Stars of David: Prominent Jews Talk About Being Jewish* by Abigail Pogrebin, p. 93.

pp. 52–53 "Every day I worked . . . of your accomplishments" is from a speech Marlee Matlin gave at a Keshet dinner on March 28, 2004, which can be found online at www.keshet.org/marleematlin.asp.

Chapter 8
Top Hats and Candy

p. 55 "As a thirteen-year-old . . . my bar mitzvah" is from *Stars of David: Prominent Jews Talk About Being Jewish* by Abigail Pogrebin, p. 220.

pp. 56–57 Practices in Morocco, Algeria, Libya, and Tunisia, are from *Bar Mitzvah: A Guide to Spiritual Growth* by Marc-Alain Ouaknin and Françoise-Anne Menager, pp. 335–39.

Index